Compose yourself!

The indispensable resource for the over-worked music teacher

Paul Harris and Robert Tucker

Contents

fabermusic.com/composeyourself

© 2003 by Paul Harris and Robert Tucker
First published in 2003 by Faber Music Ltd
3 Queen Square London WC1N 3AU
Music processed by David Perkins
Illustrations by Harry Venning
Design by Nick Flower
Printed in England by Caligraving Ltd
All rights reserved

ISBN 0-571-51990-3

To buy Faber Music publications or to find out about the full range of titles available
please contact your local music retailer or Faber Music sales enquiries:

Faber Music Limited, Burnt Mill, Elizabeth Way, Harlow, CM20 2HX England
Tel: +44 (0)1279 82 89 82   Fax: +44 (0)1279 82 89 83
sales@fabermusic.com   fabermusic.com

FABER ff MUSIC

INTRODUCTION

The act of composition can be as broad and deep as the imagination will allow. That said, learning to compose still requires a considerable degree of technical understanding. This means that the teaching and learning processes require method and a sense of progression, ultimately achieved by revisiting and connecting concepts in different ways. This book is therefore not a prescriptive scheme of work, but a collection of lesson plans which may either be 'dipped into', or followed as a course.

As we know, music is highly subjective—musicians have profoundly varying conceptions of what they like and dislike. However, as broad-minded teachers of composition, it may be helpful to bear the following points in mind:

- Anyone can compose.
- Composers feed off both their imaginations and their intellects.
- Fundamentally, it is highly questionable to deem one piece of music, or one style of music *better*, per se, than another; similarly, to assert that one composer is *better* than another.
- Though learning to compose can often seem an intimidating, even frighteningly complex task, it is also an immensely fulfilling one!

Using this book

This book is divided into 50 lesson plans or 'focuses', arranged in three sections. Sections 1 and 2 have an associated workbook, covering Focus 1–24 (excluding Focus 3 and 14); this will help structure pupils' work, build up a useful library of ideas and act as a record of their initial exploration into the world of composition. By Section 3, with the aid of a manuscript book and/or music software, pupils will be thinking and working independently towards their own personal style—be it jazz, pop, 'classical', experimental or through the rich diversity of their own musical culture.

One focus may take up a single lesson whilst others may form the basis for longer-term projects. As lessons inevitably develop in all sorts of unexpected directions, we should always be prepared to extend, revisit or change course. Class discussions should flow, with open-ended questions to encourage lateral thinking—avoid searching for one particular answer.

The two-pronged strategy

Improvisation is a very important and essential activity for the young composer. Sitting at the keyboard (even with minimal technique), the young composer will create a library of ideas, or musical 'vocabulary', that he or she will be able to draw upon as compositional skills develop. For the purpose of this book, we call this doodling 'free improvisation'. Encourage your pupils to improvise as often as possible!

However, free improvisation is essentially a right-brain activity and is only part of the story. By imposing some rules (hence accessing the left brain) we create 'structured improvisation', and begin moving from pure improvisation to composition. Perhaps the ideal teaching strategy for young composers is therefore two-pronged:

- Learning the rules of musical composition, eventually equipping them with the means to produce music of real sophistication.
- Exploring musical ideas through both structured and unstructured improvisation.

Intelligent listening

Aspiring composers must listen to a diversity of music, and listen intelligently. Each week we should expect pupils to listen to at least one piece of music and write about or discuss what they heard. Make your pupils aware of basic and more sophisticated compositional devices (as appropriate). Such frequent listening and 'aural observation' of how other composers' compositional processes work is invaluable.

Graphic notation

Graphic notation is useful for scoring special musical effects or directions for loosely structured improvisation and aleatory music (often alongside conventional staff notation). However, try to avoid the conception that it is an easier alternative to staff notation—the latter is, after all, just another form of graphic notation.

Music technology

Technology can encourage pupils to become independent learners; through editing, refining and continual aural monitoring of their work they will begin to establish a musical process for composing. Additionally, notating their music in a professional way will both enthuse and stimulate their interest. Encourage pupils to visit relevant websites: *fabermusic.com/composeyourself* offers invaluable support material and is an interactive learning tool. Additionally, pupils may wish to share their music interactively on the internet and/or have it marked via email.

Only connect …

Above all, encourage an integrated approach to composing, listening and performing: make the connections and your pupils will begin to develop real musical insight.

SECTION 1 **Laying the foundations**

 *What is composing?*

FREE IMPROVISATION Ask pupils (individually and in groups) to improvise music that depicts different colours: other pupils then try to guess the colour.

DISCUSSION How do composers create music? What is music? What does music communicate? Does a piece of music need to be memorable?
How does a composer differ from a poet, writer, artist or drama director?
Do you need imagination to compose? What is imagination?
How did pupils try to depict the different colours?

LISTENING Introduce 'intelligent listening' (see *Introduction*, page 2): No.1 from *Musica ricercata*, GYÖRGY LIGETI; *Stimmung*, KARLHEINZ STOCKHAUSEN; *Concerto for Orchestra*, BÉLA BARTÓK; any one of *Sequenza I–IX*, LUCIANO BERIO; 'Speak to me' (opening) from *Dark side of the moon*, PINK FLOYD; *Terror and Magnificence*, JOHN HARLE; any track from *Sketches of Spain*, MILES DAVIS and GIL EVANS; any track by TALVIN SINGH or NITIN SAWNHEY; any similar piece.

STRUCTURED IMPROVISATION Ask pupils to improvise on one note creating as much variety as possible. Discuss the results. Which musical elements supply the means for this variety? Now try to depict a colour again, using only one note! Explore various sound colours using different instruments and, if available, the parameters of multi-timbral keyboards, synthesisers or samplers.

PRACTICAL ① Write a paragraph on 'What do composers do?'
Pupils' workbook page 2 ② Intelligent listening (see *Introduction*, page 2).
③ Improvise music with as much variety as possible, using only two notes.
④ Again, improvise freely, trying to depict more colours.

FOCUS *Tempo, pulse, metre and rhythm*

DISCUSSION   What do each of these terms mean? (An Editor/Sequencer may be used to illustrate rhythm visually, together with keyboard rhythm styles.)

RULES/NOTATION   Discuss and compare time signatures (through conducting or other movement, listening, reference to pieces pupils may have played and so on). Introduce various note values and their rests, and show how they are notated.

IMPROVISATION   Individually, or in groups, improvise rhythmic pieces by clapping, using percussion instruments, keyboards/sequencers, percussion pads or voices. Encourage pupils to conduct.

LISTENING   *Drumming*, STEVE REICH; First movement from Symphony No.15, DMITRY SHOSTAKOVICH; examples of non-western drumming or any strongly rhythmic music.

PRACTICAL
Pupils' workbook page 3   Compose a short piece for a side-drum or other non-tuned percussion instrument, electronic keyboard or voice. It should last between eight and sixteen bars and use rhythms discussed in the lesson. Include rests. Group work might include layering on a computer, sequencer or portable multi-track.

FOCUS *Pitch*

DISCUSSION   Identify naturally occurring pitch sources (for example: bird song, engines, vacuum cleaners). What is the difference between pitched sound and noise? List pitched and non-pitched musical instruments (western and non-western). Does music need pitch? Discuss the quality of high and low sounds. How are low and high sounds produced? Encourage students to demonstrate on their own instruments. Involve instrumental teachers whenever possible.

STRUCTURED IMPROVISATION   Create a musical dialogue (with two pupils at one piano, or using a high and low instrument/voice) between, for example: a high- and low-voiced person, a nightingale and a tortoise, *etc.*

LISTENING   *Peter and the wolf* (opening), SERGEY PROKOVIEV; 'Two Jews' from *Pictures at an exhibition*, MODEST MUSSORGSKY orch. MAURICE RAVEL; *Carnival of the Animals*, CAMILLE SAINT-SAËNS; or an Indian raga. Discuss the use of pitch in the context of the piece.

PRACTICAL
(no worksheet provided)   Explore high and low pitches. Use interactive CD ROMs, sampled sounds, unusual instruments and electronic keyboards. Improvise, contrasting high and low sounds. Involve the Physics department if appropriate. Draw up a list of high- and low-pitched instruments.

FOCUS 4 *Simple melody-writing (the four-bar phrase)*

DISCUSSION What makes a good melody? (Choose some for discussion). Play/sing *Happy Birthday to you*, the theme from *Eastenders* or any other suitable example. Discuss the use of repetition, shape, balance, melodic direction and silence.

LISTENING Any good tune! For example: *Yesterday*, THE BEATLES; Clarinet Quintet in A K.581, WOLFGANG AMADEUS MOZART; *Danny Boy*, ANON.; *Away in a manger*, WILLIAM KIRKPATRICK; *Misty*, JOHNNY BURKE and ERROLL GARNER.

IMPROVISATION The teacher improvises two-bar phrases (the question) and pupils improvise a two-bar answer. Begin with stepwise movement, exploring other intervals as pupils become more confident. Are certain notes more effective for beginnings and endings? Is there such a thing as 'musical gravity'? Can this influence melodic shape and direction? Improvise question and answer phrases in pairs and groups, creating backing tracks if appropriate.

RULES/NOTATION Notation of the following notes:

Discuss the qualities of a successful four-bar phrase: rise and fall (or fall and rise!), consistency of style and content, *etc.*

PRACTICAL
Pupils' workbook page 4
Compose a number of four-bar melodies in question-and-answer form (perhaps for different instrumentalists/singers in the class), using mostly stepwise movement. Include dynamics and phrase markings. Use the notes introduced in the lesson and begin and end on C. Suggest that each tune be given an imaginative title. You may like to recommend the use of score-writing software to store and edit ideas. For non-music-readers, programme some questions digitally—the answers can be improvised.

FOCUS 5 *Developing a musical idea*

DISCUSSION Teach the class to sing or play the following melody:

Discuss its characteristics.

STRUCTURED IMPROVISATION Try the bars in a different order. Do particular combinations sound more effective? If so, why? Are there an ideal number of repetitions for each bar? Try transposing bars (perhaps up or down a tone). Reassemble the melody by choosing two bars of the original and two bars of the transposed version. Use ICT to select, copy, cut and paste.

PRACTICAL
Pupils' workbook page 5
Compose a four-bar phrase and develop the idea using the techniques discussed in this lesson. The finished composition might be eight or twelve bars in length.

FOCUS 6 — *Tonic and dominant*

DISCUSSION
Discuss the importance of the tonic/dominant relationship. Set up the school timpani (or use a keyboard or other instrument) and enjoy repeated I–V–I figures! Include a variety of rhythms. Discuss fanfares. What distinctive qualities characterise a fanfare?

RULES/NOTATION
Introduce and explain the notation of new (fanfare) rhythms and introduce perfect fourths and fifths (both melodically and harmonically).

IMPROVISATION
Using timpani (real or digital), ask pupils to improvise fanfare ideas (using fourths and fifths) over a repeated tonic/dominant pattern. Try setting this up antiphonally, with pupils or groups of pupils at different places in the classroom (the school hall would be a good place to have this lesson!).

LISTENING
Fanfares, for example: *Fanfare for the Common Man*, AARON COPLAND; 'Vision 1' from *Sinfonia Sacra*, ANDRZES PANUFNIK; Symphony No.7, HAVERGAL BRIAN; *Light Cavalry Overture*, FRANZ VON SUPPÉ; 'Throne Room' from *Star Wars*, JOHN WILLIAMS; 'March' from Symphony No.6, PYOTR ILYICH TCHAIKOVSKY; First movement from *Sinfonietta*, LEOŠ JANÁČEK; 'Fanfare' from *Façade*, WILLIAM WALTON.

PRACTICAL
Pupils' workbook page 6
Compose a fanfare using notes of an arpeggio and/or melodic fourths and fifths with a simple tonic and dominant accompaniment.

FOCUS 7 — *Simple ternary form*

DISCUSSION
Play *Twinkle, Twinkle Little Star* (or any other ternary form piece) and discuss the shape. Are ternary structures musically satisfying? Can the repeat of section A be varied? By how much?

RULES/NOTATION
How to develop the four-bar phrase into a simple ternary structure (by adding another phrase and repeating the first).

STRUCTURED IMPROVISATION
Improvise a short piece in ternary form. Does the return of the A music need to be exact? Divide the class into two groups to represent the sections. Ask the groups to create their improvisations in separate rooms, then reconvene to perform the work. Now create a second improvisation with the two groups working together. Discuss the effectiveness of each improvisation. Is it important to have a connection between the two sections?

FREE IMPROVISATION
Improvise a melody of any length including leaps (as well as stepwise movement). Begin and end on the same note.

LISTENING
'Intermezzo' from *Háry János Suite*, ZOLTÁN KODÁLY; *Norfolk Rhapsody* No.1, RALPH VAUGHAN WILLIAMS; *Ujesu Wami*, LADYSMITH BLACK MAMBAZO; *Oh so quiet*, BJÖRK; *Principia*, STEVE MARTLAND; any jazz standard; any ternary form piece currently being learnt by a pupil.

PRACTICAL
Pupils' workbook page 7
Compose a piece in ternary form. Pupils may like to add a coda.

Drones

RULES/NOTATION/DISCUSSION   Explain drones and how to notate them. Are drones equally effective as accompaniments to all musical moods and tempi?

STRUCTURED IMPROVISATION   Working in pairs, one pupil improvises a melody over a drone played by another pupil; then swap over.

FREE IMPROVISATION   Ask a selection of pupils (in secret!) to freely improvise on titles such as Insects, Clowns, Backwards, Circles, *etc.* Include drones. Others try to guess the subject.

LISTENING   Fourth movement from Symphony No.104, FRANZ JOSEPH HAYDN; any raga; *Within you, without you*, THE BEATLES; 'Fantasia on the Dargason' from Suite No.2 in F for military band, GUSTAV HOLST; anything from JOHN PLAYFORD's *The Dancing Master*; any of the *44 Duos* for two violins, BÉLA BARTÓK; suitable examples from *Mikrokosmos*, BÉLA BARTÓK; *Immovable Doh* (choral version), PERCY GRAINGER.

PRACTICAL   Compose a piece in ternary form with a simple drone accompaniment.
Pupils' workbook page 8

Contrast/Writing a March

DISCUSSION   Discuss methods of contrast: slow/fast; high/low; loud/soft; short/long; happy/sad; gentle/aggressive, *etc.*

FREE IMPROVISATION   In mixed groups of varied instrumentalists and singers, improvise music using as many contrasts as possible (include timbre as well as all the above). Discuss the effectiveness of each performance.

RULES/NOTATION   Identify and notate march rhythms.

LISTENING   A March and Trio (traditional or composed/improvised by the teacher), for example: any of the *Coronation* marches, WILLIAM WALTON; any of the *Pomp and Circumstance* marches, EDWARD ELGAR; Theme from *Indiana Jones*, JOHN WILLIAMS; 'March of the Ewoks' from *Return of the Jedi*, JOHN WILLIAMS; *The Dam Busters March*, ERIC COATES; *Liberty Bell*, JOHN PHILIP SOUSA; *The Battle of Britain Theme*, RON GOODWIN.

PRACTICAL   Compose a march with a contrasting B section.
Pupils' workbook page 9

SECTION 2 **The developing composer**

FOCUS *Repetitive compositional devices*

DISCUSSION Why is repetition important, and what purpose does it serve? What different kinds of repetitive devices do composers use? Make a list drawn from carefully selected repertoire.

STRUCTURED IMPROVISATION Individually, or in groups, improvise a selection of pieces using the techniques discussed.

FREE IMPROVISATION Find a picture or painting, previously unseen. One pupil (having seen the picture) improvises freely followed by a discussion before the picture is revealed. Did the music represent the picture effectively? Ask other members of the class to have a go. Alternatively, improvise music for a drama sketch, or (if the appropriate resources are available) improvise to a short video or TV animation. (The music may be synchronised with media editing software.) Use the above devices as appropriate.

LISTENING Repetition: *Drumming*, STEVE REICH; Second movement from Symphony No.7, LUDWIG VAN BEETHOVEN.

Ostinato: 'Ostinato' from *St Paul's Suite*, GUSTAV HOLST; *Bolero*, MAURICE RAVEL; 'Mars' from *The Planets*, GUSTAV HOLST; Theme from *Mission Impossible*, LARRY MULLEN and ADAM CLAYTON; *Eric the Gardener*, DIVINE COMEDY; *Rush*, FREAK POWER; track 1 from *Legalised*, PUNJABI MC; or African drumming.

Imitation: Madrigals by THOMAS MORLEY or THOMAS WEELKES.

Sequence: *Ding dong merrily on high*.

Canon: Any simple round, such as *London's Burning*.

PRACTICAL Compose some short pieces that include different types of repetition.

Pupils' workbook page 10

FOCUS 11 *Tension and resolution*

LISTENING *Adagio* for strings, SAMUEL BARBER; 'Jupiter' from *The Planets*, GUSTAV HOLST; 'Dominus a dextris tuis' from *Dixit Dominus*, GEORGE FRIDERIC HANDEL; *Cantus in memoriam Benjamin Britten*, ARVO PÄRT; sitar music.

DISCUSSION Make a list of ways of building up and resolving tension using musical devices: include discussion on pitch and melodic shape, dynamics, harmony, tempo, rhythm, timbre, sound and silence, texture.

FREE IMPROVISATION In groups, choose two devices from the discussion and improvise (instrumentally or vocally) a short tension/resolution soundscape. Together with another group, try working with three or four devices.

STRUCTURED IMPROVISATION Improvise a piece representing tension/resolution, restricting the melodic content to a semitone (which may be transposed, imitated, used harmonically or melodically, *etc.*).

PRACTICAL
Pupils' workbook page 11
Instrumentalists should find examples of tension/resolution in pieces they are learning and bring them along to play at the next lesson. Make a note of different types of tension/resolution scenes in TV programmes and how the composer deals with them. Compose music for a tension/resolution scene in a film, play or television programme.

FOCUS 12 *Exploring chords and cadences*

IMPROVISATION Explore three-note chords (using any notes!). Without altering the bass note (the root), change the other notes, thus creating a new chord. Now find pairs of chords that create a feeling of tension/resolution. Now add a third chord, making a series of three-chord shapes:

Tension → resolution → tension

TENSION → tension → resolution

TENSION → TENSION → tension

DISCUSSION Compare these chord progressions with punctuation. Identify different kinds of musical punctuation and how these might be achieved using chords. Introduce the word 'cadence'. Can dynamics make cadences more effective?

LISTENING Symphony No.1 (opening), LUDWIG VAN BEETHOVEN; *Also sprach Zarathustra* (opening), RICHARD STRAUSS; Symphony No.5, GUSTAV MAHLER; *Le poème de l'extase*, ALEXANDER SKRYABIN; *Brothers in Arms*, DIRE STRAITS.

PRACTICAL
Pupils' workbook page 12
Make up several short melodies, ending with two or three chords, that conclude in the following ways: dramatically; surprisingly; mysteriously; unfinished; strongly.

 FOCUS *13* *Developing a chord progression*

DISCUSSION Introduce chords, their symbols, and the idea of progression, for example: I–V–I, I–IV–VI–V or I–VI–IV–V–I. Explore ways of using chords to create different musical effects.

IMPROVISATION Create chord progressions on the piano (you might like to begin with the ubiquitous I–VI–IV–V–I!)

LISTENING Jazz standards such as *Blue Moon*, RICHARD RODGERS and LORENZ HART (I–VI–IV–V–I); any chorale by JOHANN SEBASTIAN BACH; 'Canon' from *Canon and Gigue in D*, JOHANN PACHELBEL; or almost any pop song. Try singing them too!

PRACTICAL
Pupils' workbook page 13
Using a sequencer (or multi-track facility), orchestrate the progressions adding strings, a rhythm track, guitar chords, *etc.*

 FOCUS *14* *The twelve-bar blues and the dominant seventh*

RULES/NOTATION/
IMPROVISATION
① Introduce the twelve-bar blues pattern. Improvise a simple twelve-bar blues. For the first attempts, use just the first three notes of the blues scale. Divide the bass, chords and melody between the class.
② Introduce the dominant seventh. Consider its use harmonically and as a 'colour'. What other notes can be used as 'colours'? Improvise more twelve-bar blues, this time including the dominant seventh where appropriate (conventionally in bar 9).

LISTENING *In the Mood*, GLENN MILLER; or your favourite blues recordings. Discuss how the harmonic pattern develops.

PRACTICAL
(no worksheet provided)
Write a twelve-bar blues. Encourage major and minor thirds and sixth (false relations).

 FOCUS *15* *Harmonising a tune using chords I, IV, V and VI*

RULES/NOTATION Re-introduce chords I, IV, V and VI. Explore the various inversions and discuss whether inversions change the effect of a chord.

STRUCTURED IMPROVISATION Find a way to harmonise each note of the scale of C major using these chords.

FREE IMPROVISATION Improvise a tune in C major, adding a simple accompaniment using these chords. Begin by adding one chord for every two melodic notes.

DISCUSSION What is a key? How important is the key?

RULES/NOTATION Discuss the structure of a minuet.

LISTENING Minuet in F K.2, WOLFGANG AMADEUS MOZART (or a similar simple minuet); any jazz standard.

PRACTICAL
Pupils' workbook page 14
Compose a Minuet in C using the above chords.

FOCUS 16 · *Cadences (textbook style!)*

RULES/NOTATION Introduce the standard cadences. Be imaginative! Discuss the tension/resolution and punctuation characteristics of each. Play 'guess the cadence'.

STRUCTURED IMPROVISATION Improvise short passages that end with a conventional cadence, but give each a particular character, for example: perfect cadence in a military style; plagal in a ballad style; imperfect in a waltz style and interrupted in a cheeky style.

RULES/NOTATION Notating cadences.

LISTENING Symphony No.1 (opening), LUDWIG VAN BEETHOVEN; hymns (you may like to sing some).

PRACTICAL Compose a piece that includes each cadence.
Pupils' workbook page 15

FOCUS 17 · *Fun with rhythm!*

LISTENING *Ionisation*, EDGARD VARÈSE; Percussion Concerto, ANDRZES PANUFNIK; *Veni, Veni, Emmanuel*, JAMES MACMILLAN; *The rite of spring*, IGOR STRAVINKSY; First movement (side-drum cadenzas) from Symphony No.5, CARL NIELSEN; *Take Five*, DAVE BRUBECK; *Livin' la vida loca*, RICKY MARTIN; *We will rock you*, QUEEN; Burundi or Senegalese drumming; Taiko drumming or any percussion work.

DISCUSSION Can rhythm have character? Consider pieces that use rhythm as the central impulse. Introduce irregular metre and polymetric music (two or more time signatures moving along simultaneously).

STRUCTURED IMPROVISATION Providing an array of percussion instruments (including piano), or using body percussion, divide the class into groups of three or four; each group then improvises a piece involving polymetre. Encourage the use of unusual time signatures (**5** or **7**).

RULES/NOTATION Introduce rhythmic augmentation and diminution.

PRACTICAL Notate a reference list of rhythmic patterns, for example: patterns including
Pupils' workbook page 16 triplets, rests, Latin-American patterns, more unusual patterns in compound and irregular times (including $\frac{5}{8}$ and $\frac{7}{8}$). Compose a short piece for unaccompanied side drum or keyboard equivalent.

FOCUS 18 · *Writing a work for percussion*

DISCUSSION Discuss the particular quality and timbre of as many different percussion instruments available (or use keyboard sounds). Do particular instruments suggest certain rhythms or rhythmic patterns? Do particular rhythms suggest certain instruments?

FREE IMPROVISATION ① In pairs, using different instruments, create 'conversations', maintaining a steady pulse and using the characteristics of each particular instrument.
② In groups of three, develop the idea above—try to create as many different textures as possible. If time permits, try the same idea as a quartet.

STRUCTURED IMPROVISATION   Using a larger group, improvise 'a train journey' or 'a machine'. Then try improvising a piece that gradually builds up tension through rhythmic complexity and texture.

LISTENING   *The Iron Foundry*, ALEXANDER MOSOLOV; 'I've seen it all' from *Dancer in the Dark*, BJÖRK; *Pacific 231*, ARTHUR HONEGGER; examples of scat by ELLA FITZGERALD; anything by MALCOLM ARNOLD; *Cassation in G* 'Toy Symphony', LEOPOLD MOZART.

PRACTICAL
Pupils' workbook page 17   Compose a short piece for unaccompanied percussion using a range of different percussion instruments and rhythmic devices. Alternatively, write a piece for any combination of keyboard, strings, wind or voice—treating them as percussion instruments.

FOCUS *19*   *Climax*

LISTENING/DISCUSSION   'Mars' from *The Planets*, GUSTAV HOLST; *Gymnopédie No.1*, ERIK SATIE. Do these pieces contain climactic points? How do they differ? List the compositional devices that can create a climax. Should a piece have more than one climactic point? Can music have anti-climax? Does a piece of music need a climax?

IMPROVISATION   ① Individually or in groups, improvise a piece that ends abruptly with a climax.
② Improvise a piece that contains an anti-climax.

PRACTICAL
Pupils' workbook page 18   Write a short film or TV scene that includes a climax and then compose music to accompany it.

FOCUS *20*   *Changing moods and minor keys*

DISCUSSION/ RULES/NOTATION   Introduce minor keys. Consider the differences between major and minor. Is one stronger in character than the other? Can major music sound sad and minor happy?

FREE IMPROVISATION   ① A sad piece
② An 'Egyptian' piece (harmonic minor)
③ A piece that contrasts major and minor keys

DISCUSSION & IMPROVISATION   Consider different moods (for example: happy, sad, excited, grumpy, bold, dreamy, reflective, reserved, nervous, angry, calm, aggressive, *etc.*) and then try to convey them using the same basic melodic idea.

LISTENING   Indian ragas; Oriental Noh music; *The Ride of the Valkyries*, RICHARD WAGNER; *Eleanor Rigby*, THE BEATLES; Irish folk song (for example: *Shenandoah*); or any other minor key pop song.

PRACTICAL
Pupils' workbook page 19   Compose two or three short pieces using contrasting moods, including both major and minor keys.

FOCUS 21 *Setting words to music*

RULES/NOTATION Devise a method for setting words to music (*i.e.*, read, mark the stressed words, then work out the metre, rhythm, *etc.*). Discuss vocal range; acceptable intervals (encourage simplicity here); melodic direction; word-painting. Include up-beats.

CLASS WORK Give each pupil the same poem and ask them to set it twice, to two different (but equally successful) rhythms.

DEMONSTRATION Choose one or two and demonstrate how you might add a melody to the rhythm.

LISTENING/DISCUSSION Listen to and contrast any of the following: a pop song, a folk song, a song from a show, an African call-and-response song, a song by ROBERT SCHUMANN or any other Romantic composer.

PRACTICAL Add a melody to one of the settings worked out during the lesson. Include
Pupils' workbook page 20 expression marks.

FOCUS 22 *Writing accompaniments*

STRUCTURED IMPROVISATION Using just tonic and dominant chords work out several different accompanying figures: ostinato, arpeggio, chordal (using inversions), oom-cha (or oom-cha-cha!), *etc.* Explore various spacing and textures.

DISCUSSION Do different accompanying figures suggest different moods? Find serious, humorous, dreamy, mysterious and driving accompaniments.

STRUCTURED IMPROVISATION Choose a mood, and again using just tonic and dominant (or dominant seventh) harmony, one pupil begins an accompaniment and another improvises a melody above it. Now try putting the accompaniment above the melody.

FREE IMPROVISATION Explore accompanying figures further, by using more chords and varying rhythmic patterns.

LISTENING Listen to a variety of song extracts: *The Erlking*, FRANZ SCHUBERT; *Candle in the wind*, ELTON JOHN; 'In Paradisum' from *Requiem*, GABRIEL FAURÉ. Discuss the accompaniments.

PRACTICAL Compile a reference portfolio of different accompaniment figures. Note the
Pupils' workbook page 21 mood each one suggests.

FOCUS 23 *Song-writing*

CLASS SINGING Select a variety of songs to sing (for example: *Old Macdonald*, a hymn, a simple pop song, *etc.*). Which did the class enjoy the most? Why?

DISCUSSION What makes a good song? What makes a song memorable? Discuss the various song forms. Choose a simple poem (three verses, identical music for each) to be set by the class for homework. Discuss how they are going to go about this.

RULES/NOTATION Revisit *Focus 21*, page 13. Encourage contrary motion between the melody and bass. Consider harmonic rhythm (*i.e.*, how often the harmony should change).

PRACTICAL
Pupils' workbook page 22 Using a simple harmonic shape (for example: limit the chords to I, IV, V and VI with inversions), compose the short song as discussed and set earlier. Include an accompaniment for piano or guitar.

FOCUS 24 *Changing key*

DISCUSSION Introduce the idea of changing key. Do pieces need to change key? What benefits could this have on the length of a piece?

IMPROVISATION Improvise a short, single-line melody that moves to a new key. Then improvise a melody that first moves away from then returns to the home key.

RULES/NOTATION Identify two types of key change:
① Free: simply passing or leaping from one 'key-area' to another, in an improvisational manner.
② Diatonic change (teach pupils about closely related keys).

LISTENING Prelude No.1 in C major from *The Well-tempered Clavier* Book 1, JOHANN SEBASTIAN BACH; 'Prelude and Liebestod' from *Tristan und Isolde*, RICHARD WAGNER; First movement from Symphony No.6, ANTON BRUCKNER. Discuss how each new key is introduced. Explore other music to illustrate how music can change key suddenly or gradually.

PRACTICAL
Pupils' workbook page 23 Through improvisation, compose a piece that depicts a journey. Use key changes to suggest the changes of scenery—hills and meadows, an industrial landscape, a river, mountains, *etc.*

SECTION 3 **I'm a composer!**

FOCUS 25 *Writing a TV-style theme tune*

LISTENING/DISCUSSION | Listen to and discuss various TV themes. Do they have features in common? What makes them memorable? Introduce the 'hook'. Do any include a hook? What makes an effective opening/conclusion? Discuss mood, rhythm, melodic shape and structure.

IMPROVISATION | Ask pupils to improvise the following TV-type music (or others of their choice): extremely jolly (cartoon); assertive (news bulletin); lively (sport); humorous (quiz or comedy); reflective (soap opera), *etc.*

DISCUSSION | Consider the use of rhythm in TV news programmes.

PRACTICAL | Compose a TV theme tune (but insist pupils keep their work a secret— see *Focus 26*, below!)

FOCUS 26 *Narration with music*

LISTENING | ① Select some pupils' TV themes and play them to the class. Can others guess the type of programme? (Given the popularity of this practical, you may like to move this to a separate lesson or devise a lunchtime concert!)
② Listen to *Peter and the Wolf*, SERGEY PROKOFIEV; *Children's Pieces* (with narration), ERIK SATIE; *L'histoire de Babar*, FRANCIS POULENC; or similar pieces with narration.

FREE IMPROVISATION | Ask pupils to suggest human or animal character-types. Others then improvise a short melody to represent these different characters, for example: a mad professor, a giant with a creepy snigger, a hungry lion.

PRACTICAL | Make up a short story with two or three colourful characters (human or animal) and compose accompanying music.

27 *Telling a story*

LISTENING   Listen to a short piece of programme music, for example: *The Sorcerer's Apprentice*, PAUL DUKAS; 'March to the Scaffold' from *Symphonie Fantastique*, HECTOR BERLIOZ.

DISCUSSION   Discuss ways of representing characters, events and moods by use of melodic shape, rhythm, tempo, pace, dynamics, texture and attack.

FREE IMPROVISATION   Write story suggestions on small pieces of paper (for example: 'Robot attack!'; 'Fast car ride'; 'Moon landing'; 'Building site'; 'Egyptians in space', *etc.*). Pupils pick one out of a hat and improvise a piece, while the others try to guess the theme!

PRACTICAL   Compose a piece that tells a story.

FOCUS **28** *Painting a picture*

LISTENING   'Vltava' from *Ma Vlast*, BEDŘICH SMETANA; 'La cathédral engloutie' from *Préludes*, book 1, CLAUDE DEBUSSY; 'The Little Train of the Caipira' from *Bachianas Brasileiras*, HEITOR VILLA-LOBOS; *Sinfonia Antarctica*, RALPH VAUGHAN WILLIAMS; Overture 'The Globe Playhouse' from the film *Henry V*, WILLIAM WALTON; fight scenes from *West Side Story*, LEONARD BERNSTEIN; *Divertissement*, JACQUES IBERT; *Visage*, LUCIANO BERIO; original music from the film *Groundhog Day*, GEORGE FENTON; *As others see us*, JAMES MACMILLAN.

DISCUSSION   Discuss ways of using melody, scales, rhythm, texture, chord colours, pace and tone-colour to illustrate a scene.

RULES/NOTATION   Introduce the whole-tone and chromatic scales (useful devices in musical picture painting).

FREE IMPROVISATION   As before, write suggestions on small pieces of paper, this time of pictures or scenes ('A medieval snowstorm'; 'Moonlight'; 'Waves on the shore'; 'The midnight garden', *etc.*). Again, pupils pick one out of a hat and improvise a short piece on their given theme, while the others try to guess!

PRACTICAL   Compose a piece that paints a picture.

FOCUS **29** *Minimalism 1*

LISTENING   Choose one or two short extracts by STEVE REICH, PHILIP GLASS, JOHN ADAMS, MIKE OLDFIELD, MICHAEL NYMAN, *etc.* Discuss the style.

OPTIONAL PERFORMANCE   Rehearse *Clapping Music*, STEVE REICH. Discuss the effect.

DISCUSSION   What is minimalism? How can you gain the maximum from the minimum? Why does this kind of music seem to stand still and move forward at the same time? In the music that you have listened to, can you detect any of the following: cyclical patterns; changes of texture, layers, timbre, time; cross-rhythms; accents?

STRUCTURED IMPROVISATION	① Write down a two-bar rhythm in four-time; divide the class into three or four groups. Perform the rhythm as a continuous clapping round, each group beginning a beat later than the previous. Try to maintain a single dynamic throughout.
	② Using the rhythm from the above improvisation, now add pitch. Perform this again, as a continuous round, with groups beginning after random intervals.
RULES/NOTATION	Discuss how these pieces might be notated. You may need diagrams and directions as well as musical symbols.
PRACTICAL	Compose a piece of minimalist music.

FOCUS 30 *Minimalism 2*

STRUCTURED IMPROVISATION	① Create a five-note pattern, and play this pattern continuously. By altering the accentuation (*i.e.*, accenting any particular note or any combination of notes), how many different variations can you achieve? Now include different articulation (slurring) patterns. Finally, include varying dynamic levels.
	② Working in pairs (on a piano or using two instruments), one player takes the idea above whilst the second player bases their part (either simultaneously or in canon) on the same notes but using contrasting note values, dynamics, articulations and accents. Explore these sounds and describe the results. Do any unexpected sound colours emerge?
DISCUSSION	How might minimalist techniques be combined with more conventional composition? Is *Bolero*, MAURICE RAVEL a minimalist piece?
LISTENING	'Winnsboro Cotton Mill Blues' (arrangement for two pianos) from *North American Ballads*, FREDERIC RZEWSKI; or any interesting minimalist work.
PRACTICAL	Compose a piece that combines minimalist techniques with more conventional composition.

FOCUS 31 *A suite of easy pieces 1/Modes and binary form*

RULES/NOTATION	Introduce binary form. Introduce the aeolian mode (on A) and lydian mode (on F).
STRUCTURED IMPROVISATION	Improvise waltzes in binary form, using the modes above.
DISCUSSION/LISTENING	Consider the sounds, moods and feelings suggested by these two modes. Ask pupils to perform their current waltzes and discuss the characteristics (for example, technical content, structure, range, title, *etc.*).
PRACTICAL	Compose two short contrasting easy pieces (one in the aeolian mode using binary form, the other in the lydian mode using ternary form—revisit *Focus 7*, page 6 if necessary).

FOCUS **32** *A suite of easy pieces 2/More modes*

RULES/NOTATION   Introduce the phrygian mode (on E) and locrian mode (on B).

IMPROVISATION   Pupils can chose to either:
① Improvise using the above modes.
② Improvise a modal melody over a drone.
③ Combine modes, for example: try combining aeolian (left hand) with locrian (right hand). Also, experiment with two different instruments, each playing in a different mode.

DISCUSSION   Discuss the sounds, moods and feelings suggested by these two new modes and by combining different modes. Which combinations are the most effective? Why?

LISTENING   Any modal piece from *Mikrokosmos*, BÉLA BARTÓK; *Fantasia on a Theme by Thomas Tallis*, RALPH VAUGHAN WILLIAMS; Spanish folk music.

PRACTICAL   To complete this practical, compose two more contrasting pieces (in the phrygian and locrian modes, or in a combination of modes).

FOCUS **33** *Sound and silence—finding the delicate balance*

LISTENING   ① Select pupils to perform their 'Modal Suites'.
② Symphony No.5 (ending), JEAN SIBELIUS; Finale of String Quartet No.30 Op.33 'The Joke', JOSEPH HAYDN; *Roman Carnival Overture* (ending), HECTOR BERLIOZ; 'La Donna è mobile' (introduction) from *La Traviata*, GIUSEPPE VERDI; *Egmont Overture* (last section), LUDWIG VAN BEETHOVEN.

DISCUSSION   Is silence important in music? Experience *4'33"*, JOHN CAGE. How might this piece influence the developing composer? When using silence, how do you avoid giving the impression that the music has ended? What kind of balance between sound and silence would be effective? Are there different sorts of silence?

FREE IMPROVISATION   ① Improvise a single melody-line that incorporates silence.
② Improvise a more involved piece incorporating silence.

RULES/NOTATION   How to notate rests.

PRACTICAL   Compose either a humorous or a solemn piece where silence plays an important role.

FOCUS 34   *Ground bass*

LISTENING   *When a man loves a woman*, PERCY SLEDGE; 'Chaconne' from Suite No.1 in E flat, GUSTAV HOLST; Passacaglia in C minor, JOHANN SEBASTIAN BACH; 'Canon' from *Canon and Gigue in D*, JOHANN PACHELBEL; 'Dido's Lament' from *Dido and Aeneas*, HENRY PURCELL. Ask pupils to write down a description of the musical events as they unfold.

DISCUSSION   Introduce the ground bass. Discuss the balance between unity and variety when using this device.

STRUCTURED IMPROVISATION   Work out a ground bass (for example: four or more notes, with the final note being the dominant). Working in pairs, one pupil plays the ground bass whilst the other improvises a melody line (awareness of key is important here). Experiment with different tempi.

PRACTICAL   Compose a short piece using a ground bass.

FOCUS 35   *Theme and variations 1*

LISTENING   Variations on *Ah vous dirai-je, maman K.265*, WOLFGANG AMADEUS MOZART; or any short set of clearly defined variations. Ask pupils to write down a general description of each variation.

DISCUSSION   Discuss the above. What are the characteristics of a good variation theme? Make a list of variation techniques. Here are some to get going:
① Melodic: change/add/invert notes/fragment.
② Rhythm or metre.
③ Harmonic change from major to minor (or vice versa); changing harmonies.
④ Altering tempo/dynamics.
⑤ Decoration.

STRUCTURED IMPROVISATION   Choose a well-known tune and ask different pupils to improvise a variation using just one of the techniques above.

PRACTICAL   Compose a short theme and variations. Either give the class the same theme (of your own invention!), or allow pupils to choose or compose their own. The piece should have no more than three simple variations (for example: one melodic, one rhythmic and one harmonic).

FOCUS 36   *Theme and variations 2—adding more variations*

LISTENING/PERFORMING   Listen to examples of pupils' theme and variations. Were the variations well contrasted? Were they in the most effective order?

DISCUSSION   Further methods of variation, for example: adding a second part by doubling the melody in thirds or sixths; splitting the theme between treble and bass; fragmenting the theme (possibly to include silence); moving the theme to other parts (for example, into the bass).

STRUCTURED IMPROVISATION   Choose a well-known tune and ask different pupils to improvise a variation using one of the new devices discussed today.

LISTENING   Listen to a more sophisticated set of variations, for example: any by LUDWIG VAN BEETHOVEN; or the variations on Paganini's 24th Caprice—by NICOLÒ PAGANINI himself, JOHANNES BRAHMS, FRANZ LISZT, SERGEY RAKHMANINOV, WITOLD LUTOSŁAWSKI, BORIS BLACHER or ANDREW LLOYD WEBBER.

PRACTICAL   Add further variations to the piece begun in *Focus 33*, page 18.

FOCUS 37   *Writing a mini-musical 1*

DISCUSSION   What makes an effective subject for a musical? If a performance is envisaged, stress the importance of having few characters, simple scene changes (if any) and appropriate instrumentation (for example: singers, piano and some percussion.) Discuss overall shape, for example: overture—three/four songs—finale.

LISTENING   Listen to a song (or two) from a musical, where the verse music is different from the chorus, for example: 'I'd do anything' from *Oliver!*, LIONEL BART. Then listen to contrasting songs from favourite musicals.

RULES/NOTATION   Introduce 'verse and chorus' form. Discuss key and key relationships.

PRACTICAL   Write out the story (preferably original) and decide the number of songs. Compose the first song.

FOCUS 38   *Writing a mini-musical 2*

DISCUSSION   Ask pupils to outline their stories. Are they effective? How might they use the music to reflect the story and characters? Introduce the idea of grace notes (both single and multiple). At what point would such devices be effective?

FREE IMPROVISATION   Improvise a short introduction to a humorous song—include grace notes.

PRACTICAL   Continue work on the musical—perhaps a further two songs. Include short introductions.

FOCUS 39 *Writing a mini-musical 3*

LISTENING Listen to any overture by ARTHUR SULLIVAN, a prelude from one of GIUSEPPE VERDI's operas (for example: *La Traviata*) and the overture to a musical (for example: *Guys and Dolls*, FRANK LOESSER and ABE BURROWS). Compare the approaches.

DISCUSSION Which of these approaches to overtures do pupils feel would best fit their musicals—the melody compilation or the mood-setter? Are there other possibilities? Discuss the importance of selecting an appropriate tempo, dynamics and other marks of expression. What function does the finale play? What music should be included?

PRACTICAL Compose a short overture and finale. Complete the musical, adding stage directions, scenery, props and other details. Select one or two for production!

FOCUS 40 *Rondo form*

DISCUSSION Discuss rondo form as an extension of ternary form. Introduce the idea of contrasted episodes. Does it matter whether the theme or the contrasting episodes is written first?

FREE IMPROVISATION **THE ULTIMATE RONDO** One pupil (or teacher!) improvises a short (and memorable) rondo theme. In turn, each pupil then improvises a short episode between each repetition of the theme (which is always played by the same person). Episodes can be melodic, rhythmic (played on percussion instruments, for example), or harmonic.

RULES/NOTATION If appropriate, you may like to introduce the relative minor/major, tonic major/minor and dominant minor as useful key relationships in the episodes.

LISTENING Listen to a rondo movement by WOLFGANG AMADEUS MOZART.

PRACTICAL Compose a rondo-form movement. Encourage a flexible approach to the episodes; one episode may be entirely for percussion, for example!

FOCUS 41 *New chord colours*

FREE IMPROVISATION ① Using any combination of notes, try to find chords that represent each of the following: bright, heavy, full, warm, dignified, impressive, regal, solid, thin, thick, grand, gruff, mighty, powerful and hollow.

② Choose one or two of the above moods and ask pupils to improvise in time (perhaps using five beats in the bar), with chords as the predominant feature. Now choose two or three of these moods and modulate between them using dynamic shape and tempo to assist.

③ Combine scale notes 1, 2 and 5. Play this chord—does it need to resolve? Now improvise a piece using this chord as a basis (perhaps as an ostinato in the left hand). Repeat the process with a chord built on the first, fourth and fifth degrees of the scale. (You can also try inverting these chords.)

RULES/NOTATION   For reference purposes, write down some of the chords from the three improvisations.

PRACTICAL   Compose two pieces—one calm, one aggressive—exploring these new chord colours.

FOCUS 42 *More chord colours—the seventh and ninth*

FREE IMPROVISATION   ① Play chord IV (in C major). Above it, add chord VI. Find different positions of this larger chord (keeping F as the bass). Play chord IV again and now add chord I above it. Find different positions of this new chord (but again keeping F as the bass).
② In the left hand, play the chord C E G B. Keeping the hand in the same shape play the chord on D and E. Just using these three chords, improvise a 'smoochy' tune above.

DISCUSSION   Describe the mood created by these colourful seventh and ninth chords. When might we use them? Are they effective melodically, as well as harmonically? You may also like to explore the eleventh and thirteenth chords.

RULES/NOTATION   Write down these chords. How important is it to use all the notes?

PRACTICAL   Compose a blues-style piece incorporating these new chord colours.

FOCUS 43 *Polyphonic writing*

FREE IMPROVISATION   Using a pentatonic scale, ask two pupils to improvise simultaneously (on two different instruments). Discuss the result. Now try again with three, then four pupils improvising together. Encourage the use of imitation and repetition. Was it effective? Could it be made more effective? How could textural variety be achieved?

LISTENING/DISCUSSION   Listen to a fugue by JOHANN SEBASTIAN BACH. How does he achieve variety and unity? Does he include climax and tension/resolution?

RULES/NOTATION   Discuss some considerations to take into account when writing polyphonically, for example: the relationships and contrasts between parts.

PRACTICAL   Compose a short piece in polyphonic style for two or three different instruments, using a pentatonic scale. Use music technology to edit and develop the music.

FOCUS 44 *Pedal points*

LISTENING/DISCUSSION   'Mars' from *The Planets*, GUSTAV HOLST; Prelude No.1 in C major from *The Well-tempered Clavier* Book 1, JOHANN SEBASTIAN BACH; Theme from *The X Files*, MARK SNOW; Theme from *Inspector Morse*, BARRINGTON PHELOUNG. Discuss the use of pedal points.

FREE IMPROVISATION   Improvise unusual chords (in the right hand) freely over a repeated pedal point in the left hand. Now reverse this and have the pedal in the right hand. Discuss the results.

| STRUCTURED IMPROVISATION | Improvise a piece in ternary form—the 'A' sections should be built on a tonic pedal and the 'B' section on a dominant pedal. |

| PRACTICAL | Construct a short film scene (include excitement and tension), then compose the music using pedal points. Include interesting rhythms and changes of tempo. |

FOCUS 45 *Composing a suite of dances*

| LISTENING | Movements from *Danserye*, TYLMAN SUSATO; *Le tombeau de Couperin*, MAURICE RAVEL; *Capriol Suite*, PETER WARLOCK; *Music for the Royal Fireworks*, GEORG FRIEDRICH HANDEL; Suite from *The Nutcracker*, PYOTR ILYICH TCHAIKOVSKY; dances from *The Soldier's Tale*, IGOR STRAVINKSY; or any modern dance music influenced by a fusion of cultures. |

| DISCUSSION | Introduce the various dance forms: discuss their character and structure. |

| STRUCTURED IMPROVISATION | Improvise simple examples of the above. |

| PRACTICAL | Write a suite of dances, possibly revisiting and refining the minuet from *Focus 15*, page 10 (adding an accompaniment). |

FOCUS 46 *Composing for small ensemble*

| LISTENING | Listen to a movement from a piece for small mixed ensemble (not a string quartet). Discuss the use of instruments. |

| DISCUSSION | Ask different instrumentalists in the group to give a short presentation on the range, technical difficulties, transpositions, use of articulation, particular characteristics, *etc.*, of their instruments. |

| RULES/NOTATION | Make a table of the practical ranges and transpositions (where appropriate) of the instruments in the group. |

| PRACTICAL | Choosing a small combination of available instruments (three or four), compose a short single-movement piece. |

FOCUS 47 *Ritornello form*

| DISCUSSION | In ritornello form, the rondo theme may not always return in full. Compare this idea with conventional rondo form. How else might the rondo theme reappear? |

| STRUCTURED IMPROVISATION THE ULTIMATE RITORNELLO | Improvise a ritornello movement using the same format as 'The Ultimate Rondo', *Focus 40*, page 21. Shorten the ritornello theme each time it appears— the final statement may just be a note or two! |

| LISTENING | First movement from *Brandenburg Concerto* No.1 in F major, JOHANN SEBASTIAN BACH. |

| PRACTICAL | Compose a ritornello movement. More advanced pupils may like to compose a simple concerto movement in this style. |

FOCUS 48 · *Composing a movement in sonata form*

DISCUSSION
① Introduce sonata form (as simply as possible!). How is it different from ternary form? How is it similar to binary form?
② Referring to the previous work on variations (Focus 35–36, page 19–20) discuss the various ways and means through which to develop material.

LISTENING
Listen to a movement in simple sonata form, for example: First movement from *Eine kleine Nachtmusik* K.525, WOLFGANG AMADEUS MOZART. Present a 'running commentary' as the music progresses.

PRACTICAL
Compose a simple sonata form movement. Pupils may eventually wish to add a further two movements (a slow, ternary movement and a rondo finale for example) to make a fully-fledged sonata. Encourage short and simple development sections!

FOCUS 49 · *Writing for choirs*

LISTENING/DISCUSSION
① *Adiemus*, KARL JENKINS; *A Child of our Time*, MICHAEL TIPPETT; *Unomathemba*, LADYSMITH BLACK MAMBAZO; or another choral piece of your choice. Discuss the various forms of choral music, for example: hymns, part-songs, madrigals, backing-vocals in pop music, *etc*.
② Consider aspects of choral writing—melodic shaping, part-writing, vertical spacing and vocal range. What makes effective melodic writing for voices? How does writing for voices differ from instrumental writing?

LISTENING/PERFORMING
Sing a hymn in four parts (those who can't, should play along!). Try it four times, bringing out a different part each time.

RULES/NOTATION
Revisit the harmony experienced thus far, adding appropriate chords and rules of part-writing as necessary.

TEACHER DEMONSTRATION
Compose a short setting of a poem (even just a line) for four parts.

PRACTICAL
Set a short poem or hymn for four-part choir.

FOCUS 50 · *Developing a personal style*

LISTENING
Listen to several short extracts of music by one composer. What do the extracts have in common? Discuss how these common features or 'fingerprints' forge a personal style.

DISCUSSION
Encourage pupils to think back over their compositions to date. Which ones did they most enjoy writing? Which instruments do they most enjoy writing for? Have they used melodic/harmonic/rhythmic patterns more than once? Are there any common features to the beginnings and endings? In other words, have they begun to create their personal style?

IMPROVISATION
If any pupils feel they do have some strongly identifiable musical fingerprints, ask them to improvise a piece in their own style.

PRACTICAL
Compose a piece in any form, for any combination of instruments, in which pupils begin to express their personal style.